Just Sora's Soliloquies

My name is Sora. I am your guardian spirit.

What is written in this book is just my soliloquy.

So, it doesn't matter if you believe it or not, and whether you understand it or not doesn't matter.

I just want you to accept whatever enters your mind.

I'll be so happy if any page of this book helps your life.

I'll also write explanations for the meanings of the whispering words.

I hope you enjoy my soliloquy.

Sora

How to use this book

You can read this book from beginning to end from page to page. Also, you can open one of the pages in the morning at random after taking a deep breath. This page will be the word for your day.

If you feel something or receive a message when you read, please follow it all day.

You can write the affirmation and your additional thinking down the page too.

Even same message was given to the people, they receive and feel it differently which is normal.

Please customize this book as you like it.

Copyright © 2022 by James Green
(COCORO HOUSE BOOKS)

All rights reserved

No part of this publication may be reproduced, distributed, or transmitted in any form or by any means, including photocopying, recording, or other electronic or mechanical methods, without the prior written permission of the publisher, except in the case of brief quotations embodied in critical reviews and certain other non-commercial uses permitted by copyright law. For permission requests, write to the publisher, addressed "Attention: Permissions Coordinator," at the address below.

COCORO HOUSE BOOKS
https://cocorohousebooks.com

First Printing, 2022

Just Sora's Soliloquies / James Green
(COCORO HOUSE BOOKS)

ISBN 978-0-6454912-7-2

I was born in 1968.
Since I was a child, I've always been a pacifist, never a fan of conflict.

Around 2011, I began to take an interest in the universe, and I was very attracted to ufology, the laws of the universe, and the spirituality of human life.
I listened to the various spiritualists that interested me and felt the urge to write a book about what I had experienced.

I am not a psychic or a spiritualist at all, I am just trying to understand what are the laws of the universe and the laws of the world.

It would be my pleasure If this book can help anyone in his or her way of life.

James

It is important to keep your frequency high.

Frequency is simply emitted by everything in the world. Everything in this world comes from animals, plants, stones, words, space, and air, as well as human.

Do you know you need to keep your frequency high?

This is how all people should live in this would.

Higher self is yourself.

The higher self is a higher-dimensional being with the same soul as you.

The higher self has a lot of experience in life and a lot of data.

Your higher self is sending you messages from higher dimensions to help you learn in your life, to guide you along the right track. You should let yourself receive the messages from your higher self.

Even if someone cuts you off in traffic, put it gently and silently behind you. Stop letting such things lower your frequency.

You should try to keep your frequency as high as possible. It's a waste to let small things lower your frequency. If you get influenced by others, the frequency will go down steadily. Let things go!

You are wonderful just for existing in this world.
You don't have to do anything special.

Just being born as human being is perfect. Why? Because you have a huge opportunity to learn from various experiences and grow.

What you think in your head and what you say will come true.

Did you know that thoughts become reality?

Let's say you have a colleague who is bullying you, and you either think and say, "Aw, do I have to work with that person today? I don't want to," or, "I'm happy to be able to work with that person today. I'm looking forward to it!" In both cases, you work in the same place with the same horrible person. You get the same unpleasant result if you think negatively, but you mysteriously do not get the unpleasantness if you think positively.

Why? Thoughts and the power of language bring reality to you. Try it.

Imagine you find your car broken down when you go to leave the house in the morning. Your luck will be different depending on whether you think it's your worst day, because of the car being broken down, or your lucky day, because the car broke down there at home.

You could think, "Ah, it's the worst day! Why did my car break down? I can't go to work," or you could think, "Wow! This is my lucky day! If my car had broken down on the highway, it would have been a much bigger problem."

Even if the same thing happens, it matters how you perceive it. You can perceive it negatively or positively. It is totally up to you which. If you perceive it positively, everything will go well. If you perceive it negatively, one bad thing will happen after another.

Be positive!

"Thank you" are the best words.

Try this today:

No matter what happens to you today, just say "Thank you" to everything. You may have a great day free from anger and stress.

Please say thank you for having good sleep when you get up.

Please say thank you for taking shower.

Please say thank you for the friend.

Please say thank you for having lunch.

Please say thank you for coming back to home safety.

Try it and see how it works.

Did you know that material objects have life? If you use them carefully, with words of gratitude, they will work well and help you when you need them.

We take it for granted that the kettle boils water.
We take it for granted that the car runs.
We take it for granted that the washing machine washes clothes.

Please try to talk and give appreciation to them, as below:

Hi kettle, thank you for always heating the water.
Hi car, thank you for always carrying me.
Hi washing machine, thank you for always washing my clothes.

When they actually feel your appreciation, they are so happy. They work harder and won't break. If you don't treat them well, they may break more often to let you know to appreciate their material.

Do you know why? Because material objects have souls and are living.

Don't get angry even if the car in front of you is going slowly. The driver must have a reason.

There are sometimes cars that are moving slowly. But do you know why? No, you don't.

The driver may be lost.
The driver may be on their way to the hospital with a sick person, so the driver can't drive faster. An old lady may be driving alone, so she can't drive faster.

Don't get angry when you don't know the reason someone is driving slowly. Do you wish to drive fast? You may need to drive slowly sometime to avoid an accident. You can control your driving speed with your higher self.

Also, you don't need to worry about your frequency going down over such a small thing.

Okay?

Even if you don't get the results you want, it's possible that the result is what's best for you.

For example, if you have a job interview but fail to get hired, you might be disappointed in the result, but suddenly you have an opportunity to apply to work for a better company, and you pass the interview and get the job.

We do not know the future. We shouldn't know the future. But if you do the best you can in life, your higher self will definitely guide you.

So, don't be disappointed.
Don't be let down.

Accept the reality and move on toward positive action.
That is the way you should learn how to live and spend your life on Earth.

What you do to people will come back to you someday.

This is true.

For example, if you steal money from people, one day, you'll find that your own money gets stolen, or you have to spend money on something you didn't want to.

If you are jealous of someone's success, you won't succeed.

If you envy people's success, it means you are sending a message to the universe that "success is bad." Then you will never succeed, because you think success is bad, which you created.

So, you should say, "Congratulations! Well done" to a successful person. Then you will be successful.

We were born just to experience this world.

This may be the most important thing.
When you have various experiences, you will succeed or fail, and you will learn and feel various things from those experiences.

That's how people learn and grow.

That's all life is about. Nothing else.

The purpose is not to be rich or a celebrity. The important things are how much experience you have and how much growing you do.

But don't get depressed when you fail or have an unpleasant experience. If you get over it brightly and positively, the same thing won't happen to you again, because you now know how to handle it.

So, no matter what happens, just live brightly and positively.
It is so simple.

There is no incorrect way to live your life.

Everything is correct because everything is for your experience and learning.

There is nothing right or wrong about what you have decided or what you have done.
All experience is good for you. Whether you succeed or fail, or when things go differently than you imagined, all results are correct, because everything is just experience and learning.

Think positively.

Ignore negative thoughts.

Good things will come to you.

This is an interesting comparison:

Imagine that for one whole day, you only think positively.

You wake up in the morning and are happy you have a room to sleep in.

You are happy because breakfast is delicious.

You are happy to come to work without any accidents.

You are happy you have electricity in your house.

You are happy to watch TV.

You are happy to take nice hot bath.

Now, the next day, imagine you only think negatively all day.

You are not happy because your bed is too soft and your back hurts.

You are not happy because it's annoying to make breakfast.

You are not happy because you want to get to the office early, but the car in front of you is moving slowly.

You are not happy because work is boring.

You are not happy because the power is out.

You are not happy because TV is boring.

You are not happy because the bath is lukewarm.

How do you feel? Do you feel different energy depending on whether you are positive or negative?

Negative thinking brings bad things to you.

Positive thinking brings more and more good things to you.

Why? Because the world is made like that.

If you have a nasty boss, tell your boss, "Thank you for taking care of me all the time."
Please say that even if it's a lie.
Something will change.

You have nasty people around you, right? That's natural, because each person in this world is different.

Negative energy comes to you when a person you don't like is nearby.
So, your frequency goes down.

How do you like a boss who is nasty and who you hate?

Easy! You just need to say, "Thank you for taking care of me all the time."
It is okay that it is a lie.

As soon as you say it, that boss will change, because you've already learned how to get over this situation.
Your lesson is complete!

If you regret making mistakes in the past that hurt someone, please apologize from the bottom of your heart. It will reach that person.

Did you know that the past can be changed?
I know you might say, "What?"

Okay, here is an example:
Imagine you hit a classmate when you were seven years old. Twenty years later, you realise that you did something wrong at that time.
If you say, "I'm sorry for hitting you. It was my mistake" to the classmate in your heart, the timeline changes from then on. Suddenly, that person may contact you, even though you haven't contacted them for twenty years.

You should try it and see what happens.

If anyone says something you don't like, you should think you are being given a bouquet of words.

You may think I'm saying something crazy again.
Okay, let me explain.

It is natural to get angry when someone says something you don't like, but if you get angry, they will say bad things to you again.

Do you know how to solve this issue?
You just say "Thank you" to the person. Then that person won't tell you anything you don't like anymore.

The reason is that you've learned to get over the situation positively.
That's it.

Each job has its essence. The best workers are always trying their best in their work, considering the essence of the job.

Each job has its own essence.

The doctor's job essence is fixing sick patients.

The chef's job essence is making delicious food for customers.

The cleaner's job essence is cleaning.

You should know your job's essence, then you should try your best to act in accordance with the essence.

The worst worker is one who does not utilize their skills to complete the task. People should try to do their best in their job.

I love everything about you, so you don't need to change anything.

I respect and love you. You are a great person. It's amazing just to live in this world.

So don't be depressed or worried.

You are the best as is, without any changes.

Did you know that
your happiness is an
obligation, not a right?

You are born to be happy.

If you want to be happy, you just need to think, "I'm happy."

These is no right to be happy.

It's obligatory to be happy.

You can always
overcome hard times.

I'm always with you.

All trouble should be a hundred percent solved, because this is your decision.

You decided what kind of life you want to live.
You decided what kind of trouble you wanted to overcome.
You decided what kind of growth you wanted before you were born.

That's why you can always overcome trouble.

This means that bad people were originally good people, and they are the ones who have experienced and learned in this world.

Happiness is always around you.

Happiness is right in front of you.

Think, I'm happy there is air to breathe.

Think, I'm happy I have eyes to see with.

Think, I'm happy I have ears to hear with.

Think, I'm happy I have a mouth to talk with.

Think, I'm happy I have a tongue to taste food with.

Think, I'm happy I have legs to walk with.

You see, you are happy now.

You must be happy
before you help others.

If you want to help people, you must be happy.
If you are happy, you can help others.

How do you become happy? It's simple.
You need to enjoy every moment, every day, and everything.
Now you are ready to help others.

Happy people don't feel angry.

Happy people are full of gratitude, so they don't get angry over small things.

If you are really happy, you feel peace and calm.

How could you be angry?

Try to praise the people, materials, and plants around you for a whole day. Something may change around you.

This is a little exercise. You only need to give praise.

For example:

You say to your friend, "Your clothes are nice."

You say to your colleague, "Your work is so efficient."

You say, "The leaf of that tree is a beautiful light green."

You say, "This food looks very delicious."

You say to other people, "You are so kind."

You say, "That car is cool."

You may feel something different about you and your surroundings.

Do you know that I am sometimes whispering to you?

Did you say you don't hear anything?
I understand.

Have you ever had an experience where you felt you should bring an umbrella when you were about to go out, and then it started raining, even though the weather forecast said it would be a sunny day?

Have you had the experience of feeling like you should call your friend, then your friend suddenly calls you to share some important information?

If you hear or feel something, it might be me!

If you receive and follow the voice and the feeling, you might hear it more often.

Happy people bring together happy people.

Have you heard the expression like attracts like? It is the same meaning.

This is the reason:
If you are happy, you will have an aura of happiness.
Some people can see the aura, or even if they can't see it, they can feel it.
If you are with people who have happy auras, your soul will be comfortable and calm.
Also, if you are with people who have the same aura and vibration, you will be comfortable and calm.
That's why happy people attract happy people.

It's better to be tricked
than to trick.

Have you heard this expression?

It's frustrating to be tricked, and sometimes you may suffer a loss. I hope the loss will be reimbursed, but you need to move on if it isn't. The person who tricks you will be punished in this life or in their next.

If you move forward and live positively, you will receive praise.
Then your frequency waves will be higher, which is how you grow and learn in this world.

No matter how painful
or sad you may be,
you can overcome it
brightly and positively.

It's not all fun in this world.

We are learning how to positively overcome difficulties and live through pain and sadness.

Don't get depressed. You will be absolutely fine.

When one door shuts, another door opens.

This is true!

For example, imagine you took an entrance exam for Harvard University but failed. So, you eventually went to another University where you ended up meeting your future wife.

You wouldn't have met her if you'd gone to Harvard.

This is common.

Your higher self is giving you the best path, but not all paths are fun. Sometimes you are deliberately guided on a difficult road, but it's okay, because you're just living for experience and growth.

Good things happen after bad things. This is a gift from God after experience and growth.

Have you ever experienced good things after bad things happen to you?

This is a reward working hard to overcome the bad things.

Everyone can live if they don't have everything.

You may say:

I don't have much money.

I don't own a house.

I can't get married.

I don't have children.

I don't have a good job.

I don't have a nice car.

I don't have nice clothes.

What you think you should have are actually things you don't need.

If you don't have money, you can save money and live.

The worst thing is to go lower your frequency by saying, "I wonder, if I don't have anything, is that an unlucky life?"

If you are negative, you'll get worse results and get stuck in a vicious life cycle.

It's okay if you smile; you have a happy life.

You just have to think about
how you can live happily
in this world.

For example:

You are frustrated the car in front of you is going slowly.

You are frustrated you are dealing with unpleasant customers.

This is really a waste of thinking.

You won't die just because the car in front of you is driving slowly. You just want to go faster.

You won't die just because an unpleasant customer comes. You just have to deal with them calmly.

It's a wasted action to lower your frequency when you are frustrated by strangers.

This world is a place for training how to live

If the food ordered at the restaurant does not come on time, there will be a difference between those who get angry and those who can turn the delay into laughter.

These are the same:

You may call the waiter over and get angry, then say, "Where is my food?", or you may enjoy the conversation with your friends while waiting.

Which way is better for keeping your frequency high?

Even in the exact same situation, you can spend a different time in your life with a different way of thinking, and it's free. It's just a matter of whether or not you know how to think positively.

To know happiness,
you have to
experience unhappiness.

If all the people on Earth were good people, there would be no deception, bullying, theft, stress, hatred, or conflict.

When happiness becomes normal, people don't appreciate it.

Have you ever been grateful for oxygen?
It's normal to have oxygen, so you don't say, "I'm happy to have oxygen today."

What if you ran out of oxygen right now? Everyone has to survive. You can't understand the value of oxygen unless you have the experience of losing it.
It is same with happiness.

We should appreciate things before they disappear — your parents, your partner, your own body, oxygen, your car, and so on.

Nothing is normal.
If you appreciate even small things, you will be happy for the whole day.

The cause of illness is your mind, but it's a signal that God gave you that made you get injured or sick.

There is a small signal at the beginning to let you know, but if you don't notice the signal, then it will become a larger signal, which comes in the form of serious illness.

For example, imagine you are busy with work and work long stressful hours. If God decides that you will die if you continue to work, God prevents you from going to work, at first with small signals, by making you catch a cold or making your car break down.

But if you don't notice the signal and continue to work the same way, then God will send you a big signal, a stomach ulcer, to make you realize that the way you work is wrong.
If you don't notice a larger signal, more difficult things will happen to you, so you should always feel and listen to the messages from God.
*The word of God is not related to any particular religion.

Mysteriously, everyone who has a big illness says that they have learned gratitude.

It's not natural that your body is healthy. If you don't have enough gratitude for being healthy, the illness is a gift that God gives you to learn gratitude.

There are no difficulties that you cannot overcome, because you've only set things up that you can overcome.

You may just judge something that normally happens as "difficult."

Before you think it's difficult, think, "Oh, I'm glad I have more opportunities to overcome problems and grow." If you think this way, it's not difficult.

At that point, you're almost overcoming it.

Before you were born, you decided what kind of life you wanted to live, what kind of experiences you'd have, what you would learn, and in what ways you wanted to grow.

There are scenarios of life that were set in motion before you were born.

For example:
- being born into a poor family
- becoming a famous singer
- getting married three times
- dying at the age of forty-five

For another person:
- born into an average-income family
- surrounded by normal parents and siblings
- getting married and having children
- becoming a grandpa and living until the age of 120
- becoming famous

You chose to be born to the kind of parents that best suit your life's journey to help make your life's tasks easiest for you to experience.

You were born which parents is the best to complete your scenario or task of life. You choose the parents before you are born.

The past can be changed,
but not the future.

It sounds strange, but if the past is changed, a timeline is changed too.

A timeline is time that goes from past to present and is related to emotions and events.

For example, imagine you had a fight with a friend when you were in elementary school, and you haven't contacted this friend since then. One day, you regret that because of your mistake you had that fight with your friend. You apologize to your friend from your bottom of heart.

The next day, you suddenly get a call from a friend who had a fight with you long a time ago, and you become good friends again.

Have you had this kind of experience?

Let me explain.

The timeline was that your friend hadn't liked you since in elementary school, but after you apologized to your friend, the timeline was changed to your friend forgiving and liking you again.

This is what happens!

Try it! It will work!

I don't know what will happen in the future. If you know the future, you can't have experiences, and you can't learn anything.

Often, there are people who want to know the future, but that's impossible and pointless.

For example, imagine you don't know if the business you started will succeed or not, but you try hard to find out what you need to learn and what you need to succeed. Then you learn various things about business.

If you'd known how to succeed in your business, you wouldn't have made the effort and thought to succeed. You shouldn't know anything about the future, otherwise you can't learn anything from it.

Your thoughts will come true, so you only need to think positively.

This is a true story.

Reality doesn't come first, and thinking doesn't come next.

Thinking comes first, and reality comes next.
It's a simple story. What that means is that what you imagine, for example, "Something good will happen today," and then really good things come along.

An opposite example is if you image something like, "Today is a bad day. Something bad is going to happen to me." That negative thinking will become a reality. So, you know the answer, right? You'd better think about something fun, good, and positive.

It's a simple story. Try it.

Do fun things when you have a hard time, and have fun with your close friends. Don't suffer by yourself!

Life isn't fun all the time. Sometimes you have problems. When you face a problem, you should have fun with your family or close friends. You will forget about the problem in the meantime, and you've solved the problem automatically.

What do you mean?

The problem just went somewhere else because you didn't think it was a problem. If you acknowledge it is problem, it becomes a problem. You don't need to care much. You just need to enjoy your life.

There are no problems in this world!

The meaning of living in this world is to know love.

What is love? How would you explain love?

Love for family, love for friends, love for things, love for animals. Also, love from family, love from friends, love from things, love from animals. There are various kinds of love, and the size of love is different for each person.

Having love means that there is no hatred or conflict, and people's minds are relieved and stable.
The meaning of living in this world is to know

When someone is mean to you, you haven't had enough love for the person.

This is also incomprehensible, isn't it?

Why was someone mean to you? No one wants to be mean, but you shouldn't get angry, or your frequency will go down, which is not good at all. What you should do is just overcome it.

How?
You just need to send gratitude and love to the person.

Why?
Because you are being given an opportunity to grow your soul to overcome it without dropping your frequency.
If you get angry, people will be mean to you again.

Say "Thank you" for everything all day long, even if it's a lie. You will have a wonderful day.

You can lie. Even if you are busy with work, your car breaks down, or someone is mean to you, just say "Thank you" for everything and enjoy the day. You will not be mentally tired, and you can have a wonderful day.

Try it!

If you are not determined
to do something, you will
fail. You can do anything
as long as
you are determined.

How do you get things to be successful when you do business or when you want to make other things successful?
You must believe that you will definitely succeed and do your best without giving up.

You won't succeed if you don't care or change your business when you fail.

Your business is not to make a money. It's about how happy you can make people.

Is money important? Everyone may say yes, but the most important thing in business and work is being helpful to people.

A doctor is of help to people by treating illness.

A waiter is of help to people by making the guests happy.

A cleaner is of help by cleaning to make people happy.

If you try to help others, your business and your work will be successful.

When a problem occurs, give love.

When a problem occurs, try to think that you are the cause of the problem and try to change yourself.

Send love to the person or things involved in the problem.

Try not to blame the person or things involved in the problem.
Something will change.

If you are responsible for all that happens, it's easiest for you to live your life.

The situation hasn't been solved if you blame other people or things. If you are responsible for the problem, you don't need to worry about anything, so it's so easy.

For example, imagine you bumped into someone while walking down the street.
Do you blame the person who bumped into you, or do you regret that you weren't a little more careful to avoid bumping into the person?
If you blame this person, this person may blame you, and you may get into a fight with this person. But if you try to think, "Oh, if I'd been more careful, I could have avoided bumping into you. I am sorry," then you don't need to fight, and the issue is resolved.
Then you can have a calm and peaceful day while keeping your frequency high.

The reason you are sick is because you don't have enough gratitude for your body.

For example, if you have pain in your knee, you just need to say "Thank you" while stroking your knee gently.

The pain will be released.

www.ingramcontent.com/pod-product-compliance
Lightning Source LLC
Chambersburg PA
CBHW070309010526
44107CB00056B/2538